WHAT OTHER LEADERS AND COACHES ARE SAYING ABOUT THIS BOOK:

Gail has done an excellent job in creating this resource. It is a clear and concise overview for an individual looking to hire a coach.

PAMELA RICHARDE, MA, MCC - PAST PRESIDENT

INTERNATIONAL COACH FEDERATION

This is a short, yet concise guide that helps manage expectations and chart the course for a new and successful coaching relationship. Great tips for hiring a coach for the first time and getting the most out of coaching!

ANGELA NEUMANN, LEADERSHIP COACH, PAST PRESIDENT

VICTORIA ICF CHAPTER

This a fabulous guide for leaders who are considering executive coaching. It explains what executive coaching is, provides direction on selecting a coach and offers great tips for getting the most from coaching.

NICHOLE GRENIER, SENIOR CONSULTANT, LEADERSHIP CENTRE

BC PUBLIC SERVICE AGENCY

Finally, a 'how to' for coaching that explains everything a client needs to know about what we do. A brilliant time saver and a must for anyone contemplating coaching for themselves or their organization.

TERREEIA RAUFFMAN, CERTIFIED EXECUTIVE COACH

The suggestions offered in this little book were instrumental in assisting me in establishing a solid and successful relationship with my coach. I better understood the nature of coaching as well as the expectations for taking responsibility for my own growth and development. Thanks Gail

ASSISTANT DEPUTY MINISTER, BC PUBLIC SERVICE

BE COACHED TO SUCCESS

A Guidebook for Leaders

MAXIMIZING YOUR COACHING RELATIONSHIP

Gail H. Gibson, Ph.D.

Leadership in Action Inc.

Victoria, BC

Order this book online at www.trafford.com/07-3015
or email orders@trafford.com

Most Trafford titles are also available at major online book retailers.

Note for Librarians: A cataloguing record for this book is available from Library
and Archives Canada at www.collectionscanada.ca/amicus/index-e.html

Printed in Victoria, BC, Canada.

ISBN: 978-1-4251-6523-9

*We at Trafford believe that it is the responsibility of us all, as both individuals
and corporations, to make choices that are environmentally and socially sound.
You, in turn, are supporting this responsible conduct each time you purchase a
Trafford book, or make use of our publishing services. To find out how you are
helping, please visit www.trafford.com/responsiblepublishing.html*

*Our mission is to efficiently provide the world's finest, most comprehensive
book publishing service, enabling every author to experience success.
To find out how to publish your book, your way, and have it available
worldwide, visit us online at www.trafford.com/10510*

 www.trafford.com

North America & international
toll-free: 1 888 232 4444 (USA & Canada)
phone: 250 383 6864 ♦ fax: 250 383 6804 ♦ email: info@trafford.com

The United Kingdom & Europe
phone: +44 (0)1865 722 113 ♦ local rate: 0845 230 9601
facsimile: +44 (0)1865 722 868 ♦ email: info.uk@trafford.com

10 9 8 7 6 5 4 3 2

CONTENT

"I believe that exploring and maximizing the gift of potential is what we are here to do. Having a coach to facilitate this process within us is the secret to navigating the complexity and confusion many of us experience in all aspects of our lives."

MYREENE TOBIN

BE COACHED TO SUCCESS

A Guidebook for Leaders

MAXIMIZING YOUR COACHING RELATIONSHIP

—

Gail H. Gibson, Ph.D.

Leadership in Action Inc.

"Coaching is not about teaching the caterpillar to fly, it's about creating the opening for it to see the possibility."

JAMES FLAHERTY

1

ABOUT COACHING

THIS BOOK IS FOR LEADERS

Coaching has proven its value as a leadership development strategy. Whereas only a few years ago it was primarily used to help leaders in trouble, today coaching is proactive and heavily focused on helping already successful leaders to be even more successful.

> *"Between 25 percent and 40 percent of Fortune 500 companies use executive coaches."*
> - THE HAY GROUP

This book is not for coaches. It is for you, the business or organizational leader. It is directed at helping you to contract and work with a coach, so that you can get the greatest possible value from the coaching process.

THE BENEFITS OF BEING COACHED

Coaching can help you expand your capacity to take effective action, and bring about improvement in your organization. It is a collaborative relationship focusing on your commitment to achieving business results, and to developing your ca-

> *"Asked for a conservative estimate of the monetary payoff from the coaching they got, these managers described an average return of more than $100,000, or about six times what the coaching had cost their companies.*
> - FORTUNE, 2/19/01

pability as a leader. It is catalytic and helps you to help yourself. Akin to the gift that keeps on giving, the benefits of coaching are passed on to others in the organization (e.g., your direct reports, peers). These benefits far outlast the actual coaching process.

A CHECKLIST FOR THINKING ABOUT WHAT YOU WANT FROM COACHING

As the coachee (that's you) it is important to think through exactly what you would like to get from your investment of time and money. Examples of focus areas or themes for coaching include:

☐ Expanding your influence

> e.g., creating effective relationships, leveraging your expertise

☐ Building organizational capacity

> e.g., leading creativity and innovation, creating a performance culture

☐ Uncovering your blind spots

> e.g., developing more self awareness about your mental models, perspectives, approaches, and biases

☐ Developing specific skills

> e.g., presentation skills, negotiation skills, conflict management skills

☐ Challenging your career or business strategy

> managing work-life balance, planning next career step or direction

In general, good coaching can lead to better decisions, more ideas and options, greater innovation, clearer goals and roles, support for performance improvement of self and others, and overall sound leadership development.

It is also important to be clear on whose agenda (you or your coach's) is leading the relationship. As previously mentioned, coaching is a collaborative relationship with the coach acting as a catalyst to draw out a client's full potential. Coaching is NOT therapy, counselling, mentoring, training, advice giving or camouflaged consulting. So what's the difference?

DISTINCTIONS

Coaching is not about giving the client the answers or advice - a coach works as a catalyst to assist individuals expand their own capacity to learn and take effective action. The client has the answers, is responsible for the results, and coaching is client driven. Coaching is forward oriented. Coaching tends to work with individuals who are already successful and want to bridge the gap to their next level of success.

Consultants usually bring a particular expertise to the table, are problem solvers, and tell people what to do. They have a specific agenda and drive for results – usually what they believe to be best in the situation. Consultants can succeed without being collaborative and usually consult for a shorter period of time.

Counselling and Therapy deal with the past, traumatic and clinical issues.

Mentoring is internal, usually industry specific, related directly to career advancement (how to position for promotion and success). A mentor attempts to make you more like them. A coach attempts to make you more like you!

Now, let's take a look at what you might consider in getting ready for coaching.

 NOTES:

WHAT SPECIFICALLY MIGHT I WANT TO HIRE A COACH FOR??

"Growth and development are inevitable, it's just a lot faster with a coach."

SALLY GLOVER

2

GETTING READY FOR COACHING

This chapter is designed to assist you in establishing your focus for coaching as well as other considerations in getting started, such as having a compelling reason to be coached, and being coach-able.

1. WHAT IS YOUR FOCUS FOR COACHING?

Check (√) the appropriate focus or write in where space is provided below:

- ☐ Developing goals?
- ☐ Support in achieving your goals?
- ☐ Stretching and developing your capacity as a leader?
- ☐ Personal development – who you have to be to attain your goals?
- ☐ Handling a current problem?
- ☐ Accountability partner?

AND, it's OK if you don't know, right now, exactly what you want to focus on - this would be a great foundational conversation to have with your coach.

Now that you've decided on coaching, let's consider how to find the right coach.

NOTES:

WHAT SPECIFICALLY MIGHT I WANT TO FOCUS ON
WITH MY COACH ?

2.   OTHER CONSIDERATIONS IN GETTING STARTED

Have a compelling reason to be coached:

Being coached is rewarding and energizing, but it's also hard work. Nobody does it just for fun. You must have your own *internal motivation* for wanting coaching. It's not enough that your boss tells you to "get some coaching", or that your organization endorses coaching for leadership development. You must have a specific challenge, concern, or issue that you are trying to overcome, skills that you are trying to develop, or a particular opportunity that you are trying to take advantage of. Regardless of whether coaching was strongly encouraged by your boss (e.g., "I'd like you to do this"), offered as an executive perk, or your own idea, you must have or develop energy for making personal change. Apathy and coaching don't mix.

Be coach-able:

Both you and your coach must be "learners." In particular, you must be open to questioning your own assumptions, open to hearing difficult feedback about your behaviour from others, and possess an appetite for learning and growth. You need to have a personal focus and know what you want out of coaching. You must also be open to examining the gap between what you espouse and how you actually behave on the job. A clear indicator of success is when your capacity for self-inquiry and learning grows.

Learning, personal change, and professional growth are all voluntary – they can't be forced, even by the best of coaches. Therefore, although the first couple of coaching meetings may be challenging or confusing, you must choose coaching and commit to a particular coach. If this choice isn't exercised there's a risk that coaching gets "role played", and is thus practiced at a very superficial level. You must also have the option of saying "no" to coaching, and of changing coaches if the chemistry just isn't there.

Equally important is your willingness to look at your own contribution to a problem, and not just blame others or deal with an issue at a purely rational level.

CLIENT COACHABAILITY INDEX

ircle the number which comes closest to representing how true the following statements are for you right now. Then, score yourself, using the key at the bottom of the page. Your coach needs you to be at a place in your life where you are coachable. This test helps him/her – and you - discover how ready you are, right now. How coachable are you?

Less	More	Statement
1 2 3 4 5		I can be relied upon to be on time for all calls and appointments.
1 2 3 4 5		This is the right time for me to accept coaching.
1 2 3 4 5		I will do my work and keep my word without struggling or sabotaging.
1 2 3 4 5		I am fully willing to do the work and let the coach do the coaching.
1 2 3 4 5		I will give my coach the benefit of the doubt and "try on" new concepts or different ways of doing things.
1 2 3 4 5		I will speak straight (say what's really true) to my coach.
1 2 3 4 5		If I feel that I am not getting what I need or expect from my coach, I will share this awareness immediately and ask that I get what I want and need from the coaching relationship.

1 2 3 4 5   I am willing to eliminate or change the self-defeating behaviors which limit my success.

1 2 3 4 5   I have adequate funds to pay for coaching and will not regret or be concerned about the fee. I see coaching as a worthwhile investment in my personal and professional growth.

1 2 3 4 5   I am some one who can share the credit for my success with the coach.

_____   Total Score

Scoring Key

10 – 20 Not coachable right now.
21 – 30 Coachable, but make sure that ground rules are honored!
31 – 40 Coachable.
41 – 50 Very coachable – Ask the coach to demand a lot from you!

3. IS IT FOR YOU? ARE YOU READY FOR A COACH?

Check (√) the appropriate reason or write in your reason where space is provided below:

I want to:

- [ ] Be a more effective boss (CEO, executive, leader, manager);
- [ ] Learn to use coaching skills with my employees;
- [ ] Maximize my efficiency at work; balance life and work;
- [ ] Develop good systems to improve productivity;
- [ ] Plan for my next promotion/succession in the organization;
- [ ] Develop a professional development plan;
- [ ] Better communicate within my organization/co-workers
- [ ] Meet our/my annual performance targets

NOTES:

"A coach is a person who has you do the things you may not want to do so you can become the person you've always wanted to be"

TOM LANDRY

3

FINDING THE RIGHT COACH

How do you determine if a coach is competent and suited to help you develop as a leader? Answering this question requires some initial clarity about your own coaching goals, and the value added that a coach could bring to the relationship, your development and your organization. This chapter will provide information on the elements to be taken into consideration when selecting a coach, the types of coaching that are available, and what to expect from a great coach.

The following is an extensive list of considerations. It is presented as a guideline only for your musing- it is not about the coach scoring 100 in the interview (none of us would have any work otherwise!). What's most important to you? What resonates for you? What has you feel both confident and ready to move forward into a committed and collaborative relationship? These are the questions that really matter.

1.   CONSIDERATIONS IN SELECTING A COACH:

☐ Track record and reputation

What specific successes, at what levels of responsibility, and with what industries and companies has the coach been involved with over the past few years? Does the coach have a strong, local reputation? What do their references say about the coach's capability?

☐ Experience, education and training

What background, experience, and education does the coach offer? What understanding of the corporate environment does he/she provide? What kinds of experience has the coach had with other leaders at your level of responsibility?

Is the coach professionally certified/credentialed? Was the course content specifically designed to enable the coach to work with executives and in the corporate arena? Only 10 % of today's coaches are certified. And that said, the value of coaching credentials varies widely so *caveat emptor* applies.

And what experience does the coach have that brings **value added**? Consider such things as facilitation skills, conflict resolution skills, knowledge of assessment tools (such as the 360° instrument, MBTI, DISC, etc.) as well as their understanding and knowledge of specific methodologies to develop leadership competencies such as interpersonal/relationship building skills, team building skills and processes.

☐ Personal Chemistry

The right coach is the one that is right for you. The coaching relationship needs to be one of "high trust". Differences and disappointments need to be discussed openly as they occur. For this to happen, the coaching climate and the chemistry between you and your coach has to feel right for both of you. Communication needs to be honest and direct. You must feel that your coach believes in you, and in your potential to grow. This is all very subjective. There's really no way to measure or assess these qualities other than to ask yourself, "Does it feel right?" Questions like these require self- awareness and an open discussion with your coach.

☐ Internal versus external

Both provide value. An **external** coach has an "outsider's credibility." As such, they should be more willing to challenge, and even to walk away from a coaching contract that is not working well. An external coach might also be able to relate more as a peer with senior leaders who are often more inclined to share concerns and biases with external coaches than with other employees in their organizations. External coaches may also provide a fresh perspective to issues.

It may be easier for **internal** coaches to stay informed as coaching progresses, and to challenge you with concrete examples of successes and setbacks. There's less direct expense involved for the organization, and there's more familiarity with the unique culture of the organization and perhaps a better understanding of the organization's complexity. On the other hand, an internal coach may take the organization's culture and ways of behaving for granted, much as a fish assumes it's normal to be in water.

Coaches come from all walks of life and there are no barriers (as yet) to entering the profession. Coaches bring various degrees of expertise, strengths and biases. Again, what's important to you? What resonates with you? What has you feel both confident and ready to move forward into a committed and collaborative relationship? These are the questions that really matter. Choose wisely.

---

2.   A COACH'S FOCUS:

There are many different specialities (and combinations) in leadership coaching.

Areas include:

- ☐ One-on-one coaching for:
    - ◉ Leadership development – what specific skills does the coach offer in the area of leadership development, understanding of competencies and specific methodologies for development?
    - ◉ Feedback and development coaching – this type of coaching, which usually takes at least a six month commitment, provides feedback to, and assists the leader in creating a development plan to address specific needs.
    - ◉ Content/skill development coaching
    - ◉ Intervention
    - ◉ Career transition
- ☐ Team coaching
- ☐ Live action coaching – observing team meetings and stopping the action when appropriate to coach to the personal dynamics
- ☐ Just-in-time coaching – addressing a particular or current issue
- ☐ Other

3. WHAT SHOULD YOU EXPECT OF A GREAT COACH?

A number of personal characteristics may further assist you in selecting a coach. A great coach is:

- ☐ Able to help you reframe situations into opportunities and possibilities – this is perhaps the most important ability of a great coach. They are able to use language that moves the conversation forward without being limited to the client's "story." They bring energy, and inspiration to the coaching relationship. The coach believes in your potential, and is passionate about helping you succeed.

- ☐ Grounded in business acumen and up-to-date in leadership, strategy, and organizational effectiveness theory

- ☐ An exceptional communicator; provides direct and honest feedback.

- ☐ Seeks creative solutions and is able to challenge without making you feel criticized, or "bad and wrong."

FINDING A COACH

Consider talking to your HR department for information and leads as well as your colleagues (you may be surprised at how many leaders actually work with a coach). Most cities have a local ICF (International Coaching Federation) chapter and post a coach referral service on their web site. Other national organizations that offer a coach referral service include Coach U and Coachville.

www.coachfederation.org
www.coachu.com
www.coachville.com

Now you have the right coach, how do you manage the coaching process and the coaching relationship?

NOTES:

WHAT ATTRIBUTES, TYPES OF COACHING AND VALUE ADDED WOULD I BE LOOKING FOR IN A COACH?

"Be responsible for your own progress. Remember, if there's no tension or discomfort in your coaching, you're not stretching."

TERREEIA RAUFFMAN

4

MANAGING THE COACHING PROCESS

There are two components to managing the coaching process – creating the coaching contract and managing the process itself. Managing the process would include what **you** need to bring to the contract, determining shared responsibilities, and an overview of the first meeting expectations.

A. THE COACHING CONTRACT

As the client, you should take a lead role in drafting the coaching contract, know what you what and know what is important. Although coaching is a "soft skill," measurable goals and outcomes are necessary to establish in the coaching contract. Other considerations will provide a framework of operation that will provide both you and your coach the guidelines for successful interaction. Here are some of the items you should be discussing for inclusion:

Medium: Would I prefer to be coached in person or via telephone?

Frequency: How long should the sessions be? What would work best for my busy schedule? How many sessions per month? What happens if I go on holiday or have to be away on business?

Confidentiality: When a coach is brought into an organization, confidentiality for the coachee or team is critical. To what extent is the information that is discussed in the coaching relationship to be shared with the person who does the hiring? What process, if any, needs to be put into place to accommodate this?

Consider the following levels of confidentiality:

Level 1 – Complete confidentiality. Nothing is shared outside of the coach-client relationship.

Level 2 – Tight confidentiality. Coach reports to the appropriate person in the organization after client signs off on all reports. Or, alternately, the coachee writes up a report that the coach signs off on. This degree of confidentiality may provide the client with a greater sense of control and make it safer to be completely honest with the coach.

Level 3 – Limited confidentiality. Coach reports to the appropriate person in the organization but only on specific issues requested by management. The coach is available to meet with the client and client's manager periodically.

Rates: Expect to pay $150 - $500 an hour or $500 to $1500 monthly. Fees will vary based on a number of things including the experience, training and reputation of the coach, whether the coaching takes place in person or by phone, the frequency, the number of people being coached in the same organization and the overall length of the contract. Most coaches will negotiate. Be aware that most coaches will request a three month minimum as it often takes this long to establish a solid foundation and begin to see any discernable results.

Expectations: Establishing measurable goals and outcomes is critical to the success of the coaching relationship. These should be discussed in the initial interview and included in the contract. Periodical assessments of progress are an integral part of the successful process.

NOTES:

WHAT KEY POINTS WOULD BE IMPORTANT FOR ME TO INCLUDE IN THE CONTRACT?

B.   THE COACHING PROCESS

1.   WHAT DO *YOU* NEED TO BRING TO THE RELATIONSHIP?

Giving some thought to how you want to be coached, or for that matter, how you don't want to be coached is invaluable as you undertake your coaching relationship. There are many coaching styles and approaches that fall along a continuum from aggressive or firm to gently nudging or passive. Consider, how do you best learn? Do you need to be stretched or would you prefer a laissez faire relationship with your coach? Would it be OK for your coach to push you when you feel uncomfortable or would you have boundaries about where it is OK and not OK to push?

Coaching success requires a strong and collaborative coaching relationship with both parties committed to tangible change and improvement. To maximize the coaching relationship and get the most out of coaching, you are responsible for:

- ☐ Selecting your coach.
- ☐ Clarifying coaching goals, setting the coaching agenda, and directing the coaching process.
- ☐ Giving the coaching relationship and process time to develop, and to demonstrate results.
- ☐ Keeping an ongoing journal of coaching discussions, agreements, and progress.
- ☐ Being open, truthful, and direct during coaching meetings.
- ☐ Being open to difficult challenges from the coach, and to challenging your own assumptions, beliefs, and ways of working.
- ☐ Taking a reasonable level of risk and experimenting with new leader-

ship behaviours on the job.

☐ Taking coaching goals seriously and following through on assignments.

☐ Keeping your immediate supervisor/manager informed of coaching progress (where applicable).

2. WHAT IS "SHARED" RESPONSIBILITY?

As coaching takes place on company time and at company cost, both you and the coach have an obligation to the organization as a whole, as well as to each other, to achieve meaningful progress. You are both individually and jointly responsible for:

1. contracting goals and measurable outcomes

2. determining milestones

3. regular evaluations and assessments

4. terminating the coaching process once it is no longer providing significant benefits to you. This would include openly discussing the reasons for the termination.

Both you and your coach are held accountable via regular evaluations. It is challenging to change ingrained and long-standing practices and ways of operating in business. You and your coach need to "take stock" of coaching progress from time to time; triumphs and setbacks are inevitable as you both work to overcome outdated ways of thinking and behaving. Sharing those triumphs and setbacks with your coach enhances your victories and provides a source of support during times of discouragement.

3.   THE FIRST MEETING

In laying the foundation for a successful coaching relationship, the three key outcomes of the first coaching session are:

1- Discussing mutual expectations
2- Determining how best to work with each other to maximize the benefits of the coaching process
3- Establishing a benchmark for improvement (defining success)

The initial meetings serve as both an opportunity for you and the coach to get to know one another and to get an early sense of how coaching can assist you in your development. The first focus needs to be on assessment and benchmarking. Realistically defining success provides a foundation and direction for the coaching process.

Now that you are managing the coaching relationship, how do you measure value?

NOTES:

WHAT COMMITMENTS WOULD I MAKE TO THE COACHING RELATIONSHIP?

"Any team that is not keeping score is just practicing."

YOGI BERRA

5

MEASURING VALUE

H ow will you know that coaching is working? There are many opportunities, both subjective and objective, available to assist you in determining the value of coaching.

These include:

a) Assessing progress toward the goals set out in the coaching contract

b) Conducting a comparative 360° assessment

c) Interviewing or surveying your direct reports and peers – has there been a perceived difference in your leadership behaviours – what has the impact been?

d) Have you maintained regular assessments and adjusted your goals accordingly?

e) How you *feel* about the value of your coaching relationship? For example, do you feel encouraged? In action and ready to move forward? Proud of your accomplishments? Looking forward to your sessions? Confident, empowered, energized?

NOTES:

HOW MIGHT I MEASURE VALUE?

"Step up to your best self; make proactivity and possibilities daily habits."

STEPHEN COVEY

6

CONTINUING YOUR DEVELOPMENT AFTER COACHING

Ending the coaching relationship doesn't mean you end your development. As a last step in coaching, work with your coach to put together a personal development or "game" plan to support your ongoing learning and growth. It should include measures, and accountability. Will your coach be available for informal sessions or formally scheduled sessions once every 3 to 6 months?

Checklist of things you will do after coaching:

- ☐ Establish goals, actions and timelines
- ☐ Create a personal learning plan
- ☐ Determine how often you will work with your formal coach
- ☐ Decide on informal coaching relationships – will you "deputize" a colleague to work with you as a peer coach or coaching buddy?

NOTES:

WHAT DO I NEED TO INCLUDE IN MY PERSONAL PLAN FOR ONGOING DEVELOPMENT?

CONCLUSION

I hope that you have benefited from using this guidebook. I also hope that I have met the promise set out in chapter 1 – to assist you to contract and work with a coach, enabling you to get the best possible value from the coaching process. You've made a great decision and I wish you every success in working with your coach towards your full leadership capability.

Gail

*"Coaching is nothing but
an ongoing conversation
about achieving something
previously difficult or
impossible."*

ROBERT HARGROVE

Gail is passionate about working with leaders who are authentic, self aware, courageous, innovative, and inspiring – leaders who are people centered and excited to lead differently. Employee engagement is a function of the way an organization is led and the way that leadership is translated into daily management practices. Everyone has the potential to be a leader – not everyone chooses to be one. Being a leader is not the same as doing leadership. Conscious leadership is a choice. Gail's commitment is to support leaders by recognizing, celebrating, and leveraging their strengths. Full leadership potential can be fulfilled when leaders understand that their choices matter, their actions make a difference, and their role modeling influences others. Gail provides direct, honest feedback, and serves as a catalyst for individuals to explore and make the most of their own experience and wisdom.

Before pursuing a doctorate in 1990, Gail gained 15 years of executive-level, practical experience in the public, private, and not-for-profit sectors that enriches her coaching and leadership development practice. As an executive director of several national not-for-profit organizations, consultant/coach to senior executives and managers of global corporations as well as municipal governments, Gail evolved a successful approach to increasing organizational, team, and individual leadership effectiveness that transforms culture, empowers employees, and makes change work. Gail's background provides a deep appreciation for the challenges facing organizations today and contributes richness to her coaching and facilitation skills.

Gail has a Ph.D. in Organizational Behaviour and was a founding faculty member in the design and delivery of the Master's in Leadership Program at Royal Roads University. In addition to her private practice, Gail also delivers a number of the modules for the BC government's "Leading the Way" initiative. In 2001, Gail co-founded, designed and delivered the Executive Coaching Certificate Program at Royal Roads University in Victoria, B.C. Gail is a graduate coach of CCUI and a certified facilitator of the Coaching Clinic™.

Gail H. Gibson, Ph. D.
Leadership in Action Inc.
250.744.4310
ghgibson@shaw.ca
www.leadershipinactiongroup.com